Richard Morris Hunt:
The Collector

Richard M. and Catharine H. Hunt townhouse interior,
New York (detail), S. Beer, colored stereoscope, ca.1865.

Richard Morris Hunt
THE COLLECTOR

Reflections on Collecting by Richard M. and Catharine H. Hunt

Sam Watters

APPLEWOOD BOOKS

Published in cooperation with The Preservation Society of Newport County for its exhibition *Richard Morris Hunt: In a New Light* at Rosecliff, May–November 2025.

ISBN 978-1-4290-0604-0

Library of Congress Control Number: 2025933733

Published by Applewood Books,
an imprint of Arcadia Publishing

Charleston, South Carolina

Contents

Catharine, Richard M. and Richard H. Hunt, Paris;
Richard M. Hunt, sketchbook page, 1862.

Richard Morris Hunt

b. Brattleboro, Vermont, 1827
d. Newport, Rhode Island, 1895

Lived in Paris and studied at the École des Beaux-Arts, 1846-1855

Married Catharine Clinton Howland (1841-1909), 1861

Studios and homes in New York and Newport, Rhode Island, 1855-1895

At the bequest of Catharine H. Hunt, the paper collections of Richard Morris Hunt were donated to the American Institute of Architects (AIA) in 1926; then transferred to the Library of Congress, Washington, DC, 2010

If you are lucky enough to have lived in Paris as a young man, then wherever you go for the rest of your life, it stays with you, for Paris is a moveable feast.

Ernest Hemingway, *A Moveable Feast*, 1964

N 1850, Paris was a center of western art and design. Publishers and photographers prospered with new technologies, issuing shelves of books and prints illustrating the wonders to be admired *and* acquired in the "capital of the nineteenth century."[1] Shops displayed an array of industrially manufactured goods and auctions sold elegant loot from a century riled by revolution.

Living in this bazaar of luxury and profusion, devoted Francophile Richard Morris Hunt became an architect and voracious collector. From 1847 he studied architecture at the École des Beaux-Arts and sketched his way across Europe and the Middle East, recording in pocket sketchbooks buildings and interiors he discovered and the collectibles he acquired. He returned to America in 1855 to settle in New York. In rooms near Washington Square, he installed what he recalled as three thousand books on the arts and five thousand photographs of buildings, interiors, of sculpture, decoration and scenic views, acquired abroad.[2] To these collections he added plaster casts of architectural elements.

Books, photos, and casts were inspiration for the historicist architecture Richard Morris Hunt practiced, but his collection included more. He had acquired "articles of domestic use," Renaissance pottery, porcelains and iron work, "church ornaments and altar-pieces," "clocks of different ages," and "ornaments taken from venerable edifices of the middle ages." There were decorative paintings from demolished castles, "carved antique cabinets, filled with bronzes, medallions, precious glass of Venice and curiosities of fine handwork in all the arts." There were "relics of Egyptian, Roman, and Grecian Antiquity," embroideries, musical instruments, and "strange and costly toys of every era of civilization." A contemporary recalled the collection as a "museum." Not only was it a

Fig. 1. Richard M. Hunt sketchbook cover, ca. 1850.

"novelty, it was a sensation. No such thing has been seen [in America] before... there was not a museum, not even a private collection, of artistic and historical objects made for their value as works of art."[3]

Hunt's avarice as a collector continued throughout his life. Documentation is scarce but in the sketchbooks that he filled with lists and drawings we glimpse his relentless pursuit. He financed his purchases through inheritance from his landowning family, but his resources expanded after he married Catharine C. Howland. She was heir to a shipping fortune and over the years became a collector of embroideries and fans, collectibles thought appropriate for women.[4]

Like their wealthy friends, the Hunts were advocates for the past, committed to studying the best of aristocratic, European culture. Obligated by enlightened noblesse oblige, they endeavored to use what they learned to realize the "civilized" society envisioned by their colonial ancestors.

In 1867 Richard and Catharine Hunt, with their young son Richard H. Hunt, sailed to Paris where he represented America as a juror for architectural work at the *Exposition universelle d'art et d'industrie* celebrating Emperor Napoleon III's modernization of France's capital city

Fig. 2. Russia's display, Exposition Universelle, Paris (detail), 1867.

Fig. 3. Great Exhibition of 1851, London (detail), Louis-Émile Durandelle, 1851.

Désachy
Musiciens
Chapiteau de l'Alhambra
" XIIme siècle Notre Dame de Paris
Aix la Chapelle
" St Martin des Champs
Console grec
" Tombeau du Cardinal d'Amboise
Devant de Coin ... de Henri IV
Rinceau d'Allemagne XIIme siècle
" St Denis
Panneau de Venise

Fig. 4. Hunt's sketchbook list of cast purchases from Alexandre Désachy, Paris, 1867.

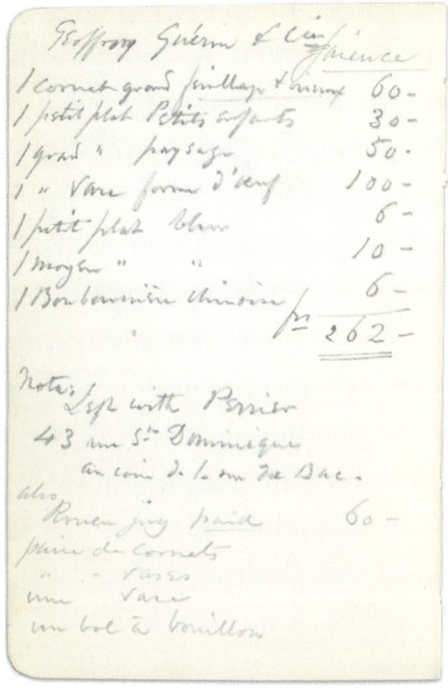

Geoffroy Guérin & Cie faience
1 cornet grand feuillage & oiseaux 60-
1 petit plat Petits enfants 30-
1 grand " paysage 50-
1 " Vase forme d'oeuf 100-
1 petit plat bleu 6-
1 moyen " " 10-
1 Bonbonnière chinoise 6-
fr 262-

Note: Left with Perrier
43 rue St Dominique
au coin de la rue du Bac.
also Rouen jug [illegible] 60-
paire de cornets
" vases
une vase
un bol à bouillon

Fig. 5. Hunt's sketchbook list of faience purchases from Geoffroy Guérin et Cie, Paris, 1867.

and its colonies. Now consumer societies, America and western countries displayed advancements in the "industrial arts" to lure new customers and boost their standing as civilizations. Leaders believed that finely designed products—crafted pottery and cut crystal, pianos and furniture, embroidered cottons and woolens—would ameliorate and refine the lives of the bourgeoisie and laboring poor.[5] These objectives were predicates to fairs Richard had already attended, including London's groundbreaking Great Exhibition of 1851.

Like the architecture Richard Morris Hunt and his generation practiced, the design of products exhibited in Paris was eclectic, with displays in iron, bronze, and marble ranging from Medieval to Renaissance Revival. Supported by their government, French exhibitors displayed marquetry, miniatures, and embroideries from Louis XII to Louis XVI, to promote private collecting and inspire reproductions that would surpass historic models.

Between his obligations to the Parisian fair, Richard Hunt did what he had done since student days at the École—he went shopping, his purchases reflecting the very didactic eclecticism made fashionable by expositions. From publishers Richard acquired volumes on the castles at Fontainebleau, Marly, and Heidelberg, on monastic architecture and medieval decorative arts. From the studio of Alexandre Désachy who sold plaster casts at retail and through catalogs to an international market of artists, collectors, and museums, he selected over fifty classical and medieval elements. Charles Marville offered photos of architecture and a leading dealer in polychromed earthenware, Geoffroy Guérin et Cie, sold Richard and Catharine Hunt housewares that were also works of art.[6]

As exuberant and fruitful as Richard Hunt's Paris collecting was, it did not stop in France. After the exposition, he and his family headed north to Holland, Sweden, and Norway to reach St. Petersburg and Moscow. As they travelled by rail, carriage, and steamer, Richard lost no opportunity to acquire ivories, silver, local costumes, a Russian crucifix, a malachite box, icons, and jewelry. On return to Paris, he inventoried his over two hundred purchases for shipment back to America.[7]

45

Antique Statue

Faun at rest, Rome
from the Museum Vatican

Fig. 6. Page from Désachy catalog, 1860.

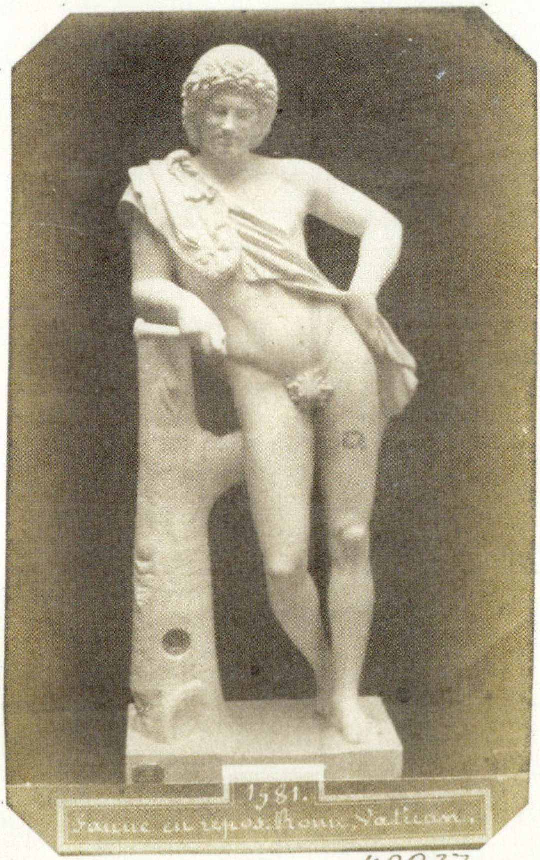

Haut.

Large.

1581.
Faune en repos. Rome Vatican.

40,937.

en Plâtre. —— Plastique.

Paris.
17. Rue de Seine.

GALERIE A^{dre} DESACHY

Londres.
49, Great Marlborough Street.

France is the only country where some small phrase could bring about a great revolution.

Honoré de Balzac, *The Human Comedy*, 1829

ICHARD Morris Hunt was a *bibeloteur*, a collector of the *bibelot,* medieval French for knick-knacks, curiosities, works of art and antiques, rare and minor, also known as bric-a-brac. Through his diverse purchases he had joined "the army of young collectors" who, from the 1830s, recognized that art was not confined to painting, sculpture, and architecture. Across the continent they acquired "weapons, furniture, silver, tapestries, enamels, faience...." Emanating from the Renaissance cabinet of curiosity, the *wunderkammer* or *kuntskammer*, their collections of bibelots were displays of imperial spoils meant to demonstrate the amateur's erudition and taste.[8]

Fig 7. Alexandre-Charles Sauvageot apartment, Paris, Arthur Henry Roberts, 1856.

Fig. 8. "Vestibule forming a Gallery," Alexandre du Sommerard residence, later Musée de Cluny, Paris, 1846.

At the time, a surge in archeological and scientific discoveries, expanding a sense of history and order, drove the development of classification systems and relatedly, new disciplines including art and architectural history. Reflecting this taxonomy, the bibeloteur curated her/his objects according to date, type, and style, like overseers of the new museums created after the formation of the Louvre in 1793. As one critic writes, in an era when the "cult of Science and the cult of Art" were intellectual obsessions, material things were at once a "source of knowledge" and "a source of aesthetic power."[9]

Richard Morris Hunt was well acquainted with his fellow bibeloteurs in Paris. Entranced by the tragedienne, Rachel Félix, he would have seen illustrations of her eclectic Gothic-to-Louis XV collections. At the Louvre were the bibelots donated by violinist and collector, Alexandre-Charles Sauvageot. But Hunt chose for particular study the "singular curiosities" collected by Alexandre du Sommerard, who had lived in what became the Musée de Cluny in 1847. The archeologist and government official had acquired hundreds of objects from the twelfth through seventeenth centuries that he displayed in ways to evoke epochs before Louis XIV, notably the reign of François I whose chateaus influenced Hunt's architectural practice, as seen at Newport's Ochre Court and Biltmore.[10]

They discussed art with enthusiasm, read, studied, and dreamed of its divine possibilities...

Henry T. Tuckerman, *Book of the Artists*, 1867

HEN Richard Morris Hunt began his career in 1850s New York, the banking and trading hub was expanding its cultural offerings to compete with Europe. His client, the financier August Belmont, and his friend, John T. Johnston, first president of the Metropolitan Museum of Art, were early private collectors, building residential galleries occasionally opened to the public. The Civil War slowed this momentum until the late 1860s, when the city resumed its ascent as private wealth rose to new heights.[11]

Hunt believed that knowing and seeing western art was necessary for America to become civilized, defined by the popular Webster's Dictionary in 1862 as that "state of being refined in manners from the grossness of savage life, and improved in arts and learning." Art was a "glorious thing," he told architects, and if the country did not take it up, "we will make it, we'll educate it...." This they would achieve by designing buildings, interiors, and landscapes, derived from canonical traditions, and by institutionalizing art through museums and professional societies.[12]

One of Richard Morris Hunt's earliest undertakings was joining twelve architects to found the American Institute of Architects (AIA) in 1857. Its mission was the advancement of architecture as an art, not a mechanical trade.[13] In 1869, on a mild fall evening on lower Broadway, Richard opened a meeting of the AIA as the president of its New York chapter. After preliminary remarks, he returned to a topic he had raised years earlier—the formation of an architectural "Library and Museum of Art." "[I]n a mercantile community like ours," he began, exploiting "the vast resources of a new hemisphere..." was a preoccupation. However, with the recent increased interest in "everything appertaining to art and to a higher cultivation [i.e. to civilization]," there was promise of progress.[14] Could it now be expected, he asked rhetorically, that "men... from an innate love of the beautiful, wealth, position or culture, take an interest in the first struggles of a new people in search of more artistic light" and fund institutions whose "influence will bear on the nation" as museums and societies did in Europe?[15] Hunt understood, with American pragmatism, that art appealed for both its aesthetic qualities, associated with moral uplift and enlightenment, and the social prestige it brought to the collector and patron, as it had to castle-building aristocrats and papal grandees.

Fig. 9. South Kensington Museum collection as first installed, Marlborough House, London, John C.L. Sparkes, 1856.

As a complement to the AIA's architectural library, Hunt envisioned for New York a "museum of art," collecting "models, casts, drawings, photographs, in fact everything referring to architecture and the cognate arts—thus forming a department such as now exists at the [South] Kensington Museum [Victoria & Albert Museum from 1899]." The London institution had opened its own building the year the AIA was founded, and had already proven, Hunt explained, to be not only "a source of great instruction to the student, but to the public at large." Its collections were based on government purchases from the over 100,000 art and commercial objects exhibited at the 1851 Great Exhibition (see Fig. 3). While selecting the best examples was a consideration, the urgent mandate was to collect representations of the industrial arts for specialized galleries, including ones dedicated to casts, photographs, and architecture, to train craftspeople in fine design. Even Queen Victoria was on board for this landmark undertaking which would further her empire's claim to civilization. "The advancement of fine arts and of practical science will be readily recognized by you as worth the attention of a great and enlightened nation," she told Parliament in 1852.[16]

Richard Morris Hunt was not alone in his quest for a museum to enrich America. A week after the AIA meeting, he was uptown for a gathering of the Art Committee of the Union League Club of New York, organized by him and city leaders during the Civil War. The "encouragement of art" was among its missions,

Fig. 10. Casts, models, and photographs in the South Kensington Museum's "Education" gallery, ca. 1859.

MODEL OF THE TRANSIT CIRCLE
ROYAL OBSERVATORY GREENWICH
SOUTHERN ZONE OF CONSTANT PRECIPITATION

and the Committee was rallying behind the "foundation of a permanent national gallery of art and a museum of historical relics."[17]

The Union League's committee chair framed the cause. Though the benefits to the "rich and poor" of Europe's museums were self-evident, the wealthy had failed the nation in this regard. Their vaunted "American enterprise and intelligence" had "effected so little in this direction," even in the richest cities.

Individual authorities at the meeting elucidated what a museum might achieve and require. The brother of Henry Cole, the leading intellect of the South Kensington Museum, articulated that institution's mission, and a Princeton professor laid out a study of European museums, noting the importance of Paris's Musée de Cluny (see Fig. 8). Richard Morris Hunt was the voice of New York's architectural community. He recounted that the AIA had endeavored for a decade to fill the "gap" in the city's art offerings. Though fund raising had been slow, the institute had successfully acquired publications for its Architectural Library of the City of New York. It remained intent on creating an associated arts museum and a patron loan program, both modeled after South Kensington. As expected, Richard lobbied for a new building to house the Union League's national museum. "When you catch a bird," he concluded, "you need a cage" to keep it. He believed that funding construction would be easy by comparison to "fill[ing] the building when we have it."[18]

The morality of art consists, for everyone, in the side that flatters its own interests.

Gustave Flaubert, *Bouvard and Pécuchet*, 1881

FIFTEEN years since his arrival in Gotham, Richard Morris Hunt had contributed to the institutionalization of art in America. He had launched an influential architectural practice, soon to include the design of libraries and museums; and supported the AIA and Metropolitan Museum of Art (Met). Later in the century, he would promote sculpture and murals in public spaces. Probably for reasons of money and social politics, the AIA's museum never came to fruition. Instead, the institute's wealthy honorary members pooled their resources to establish the Met, founded in 1870 by leaders in the arts, law, finance, and manufacturing.

Fig. 11. "Free Industrial Art School of the Metropolitan Museum." *The Daily Graphic* (New York), 1880.

These men included landscape architect Frederick Law Olmsted, sculptor John Quincy Adams Ward, and Richard Morris Hunt, who worked together in New York and Newport. With ambivalence about South Kensington's singular focus on the industrial arts, they would build an encyclopedic collection of fine art while also acquiring "specimens illustrating the application of art to manufactures" to be used in educational programs.[19] (Fig. 11) A decade would pass before the museum completed its first building, and over twenty years before Hunt designed its signature Fifth Avenue entrance.

The Met opened to acclaim in 1880, its central hall by Calvert Vaux and Jacob Wrey Mould inspired by the South Kensington Museum, as Richard Morris Hunt and his fellow members on the board's architectural

Fig. 12. Dining room, Wetmore residence, Chateau-sur-Mer, Newport, Michael Froio, 2020.

Fig. 13 (opposite). Dining room, Marquand residence, Linden Gate, Newport, ca. 1880.

committee had recommended. Galleries were lined with art, fine and applied, loaned by patrons including Richard and Catharine Hunt. Trustee Joseph H. Choate, Richard's childhood friend and attorney, presented a summa of art's power "to humanize, to educate, and refine a practical and laborious people." From seeing the best work of civilizations, public taste, and consequently profits, would rise, securing the nation's global standing. To permanently fill the Met's galleries, Hunt, a museum trustee for twenty-five years, and a member of its early contributions and loan committees, cultivated an activity he knew first-hand, private collecting. Some of his clients were museum trustees and donors, and as their architect and advisor in decorating new interiors, he could encourage the collecting of what might become museum loans and gifts.[20]

Fig. 14. Gothic Revival room, Marble House, with Gavet collection reinstalled, 2009.

The 1870s were the era of the American bibeloteur. At Newport's Chateau-sur-Mer (1852; 1873–1882), the granite mansion of merchant heir and US senator from Rhode Island, George P. Wetmore, and his wife Edith M. Keteltas, Richard Morris Hunt worked with Florentine craftsman Luigi Frullini to design and install an Italian Renaissance Revival dining room and library, both displaying bibelots. Similarly, Frullini likely collaborated with Hunt on the nearby cottage, Linden Gate (1873), nicknamed Bric-a-Brac Hall for its superfluity of objects collected by its owner Henry G. Marquand.[21]

Richard Hunt was both art consultant and architect to Marquand and his wife Elizabeth Allen.[22] The railroad financier became the Met's second president and donated cases of ancient objects to support the museum's "[t]echnical schools for the teaching of artisans... essential to the progress of American industrial art."[23] From time to time, Hunt judged student work produced in classes that included "Carriage Drafting," "Decoration in Distemper," "Modeling and Carving," "Drawing and Design," and "Plumbing."[24]

For the interior of the Marquands' New York house (1884), Hunt followed a practice prevalent in Europe, installing rooms decorated in thematic styles—English Tudor, Japanese, Ancient Greek, and Moorish—to display collections of related periods.[25] This was an immersive experience, a colonizing of selected world taste by a museum founder and collector.

1880s prosperity made Medicis of Richard Morris Hunt's richest clients, the heirs of New York transportation magnate Cornelius Vanderbilt. Their Marble House, The Breakers, and Biltmore are Hunt's most famous extant residences, all built between 1888 and 1895 to exemplify American architecture at home and to compete with peers abroad. Hunt and his clients were looking at European collectors, including Richard Wallace in London and the *objets de luxe* collecting Rothschilds whose French Château de Ferrières (1855) was disdained by the literary Goncourt brothers, as a "curiosity shop" of "crushing *bibeloterie*."[26]

Hunt's first Vanderbilt client was Alva E. Smith who married William K. Vanderbilt in 1875. Educating children was the domain of women, and Alva viewed fine homes as civilizing forces for her family and the public at large. She was twenty-five when she commissioned Hunt to conceive a François I Revival chateau (1882) on Fifth Avenue. Parisian Jules Allard and others decorated its rooms by period, with old masters by Joshua Reynolds and François Boucher, and gilded furniture by Jean-Henri Riesener for Marie-Antoinette, a taste reflecting the gradual shift from bibeloteur to museum-quality connoisseur. William K. Vanderbilt bequeathed these collectibles to the Met, a move no doubt

Fig. 15. Bedroom, Émile Gavet apartment, Paris, ca. 1889.

encouraged, both by Richard Morris Hunt, and his brother, the builder of The Breakers, Cornelius Vanderbilt II, a Metropolitan trustee and fine arts donor.[27]

At Newport, Alva Vanderbilt again enlisted the arts to project her superior culture. For Marble House (1892), an American Petit Trianon designed by Richard Morris Hunt, she acquired more old masters and installed a Gothic Revival room. Here she displayed an Italian, sixteenth-century bell and an Italian Renaissance glazed bottle, just two of the material arts from the medieval to Renaissance collection she purchased *en bloc* from the bibeloteur Émile Gavet, a French dealer and sometimes architect in Hunt's circle who had assembled bibelots since the 1860s and 1870s. His beamed and tapestried Paris apartment interiors, indebted to Alexandre du Sommerard, were a model of early museum display that Hunt followed at Marble House. As with her New York masterpieces, Alva's Gavet collection was museum bound. In the 1920s circus entrepreneur John Ringling acquired the works for both his house and museum in Florida.[28]

Another dealer known to Richard Morris Hunt was Gavet's competitor, the Viennese-born Frédéric Spitzer. Also inspired by du Sommerard and intending to create a "*Musée des arts industriels,*" Spitzer displayed medieval and Renaissance bibelots throughout his Paris townhouse. The auction of his collections in 1893 yielded the fifteenth-century stained-glass windows purchased by yachtsman and New York real estate heir, Ogden Goelet, for his Newport castle, Ochre Court (1893), designed by Richard Morris Hunt. Today they remain *in situ*, after an heir's unsuccessful attempt to sell them to the Metropolitan Museum.[29]

Parisian collections and Hunt's residential commissions in New York and Newport were harbingers of houses that became public museums in Europe and America at century's end.[30] If the encyclopedic public institution served collective interests, the house with museum-quality objects was both a monument to private identity and affirmation of the importance of art in civilized society.

Archaeology... for the young man and young woman, is the indispensable compliment of a serious education.

Paul Lacroix, *Les Arts au Môyen Âge et de la Renaissance,* 1869

IVILIZER of the rich through architecture and collecting, and advocate for artisan education by museums and professional societies, Richard Morris Hunt pursued what he recommended to the AIA in 1869. He assembled the contents for a museum of architecture and art: books, photographs, drawings, plaster casts, and related arts.

As a dedicated bibeloteur, Hunt's collecting activities were acquisition and cataloging. His wife Catharine recalled with humor Richard's Sunday retreats to their New York townhouse library where he searched for books and "fuss[ed]" over "magazines and papers."[31] These weekly respites produced the thousands of magazine clippings, stained-glass cartoons, engravings, and drawings by fellow architects and artists that Richard and Catharine pasted into scrapbooks. Scrapbooking was an archeological activity "form[ing] a taste for the best and a distaste for the bad" and so popular that the avid adherent Mark Twain patented his own album design in 1873.[32]

After Richard's death in 1895, Catharine Hunt created dozens of large-format scrapbooks, extant today. Some are bound with gold-stamped labels identifying subjects including City Houses, Decorative Designs, Municipal Buildings, Statuary and Sculpture, as well as subjects tangential to practicing architecture such as Costumes, Architects, and Furniture, Bric-A-Brac. Similarly, she and an assistant created folios of Richard's office drawings and single albums for large, residential projects.

Along with his enthusiastic scrapbook activities, Richard Morris Hunt collected thousands of photographs. He owned works by masters Émile-Louis Durandelle (see Fig. 3), Édouard Baldus, and Charles Marville as fine prints. He and Catharine cataloged stock images of architecture and interiors in over forty labeled albums. Photo

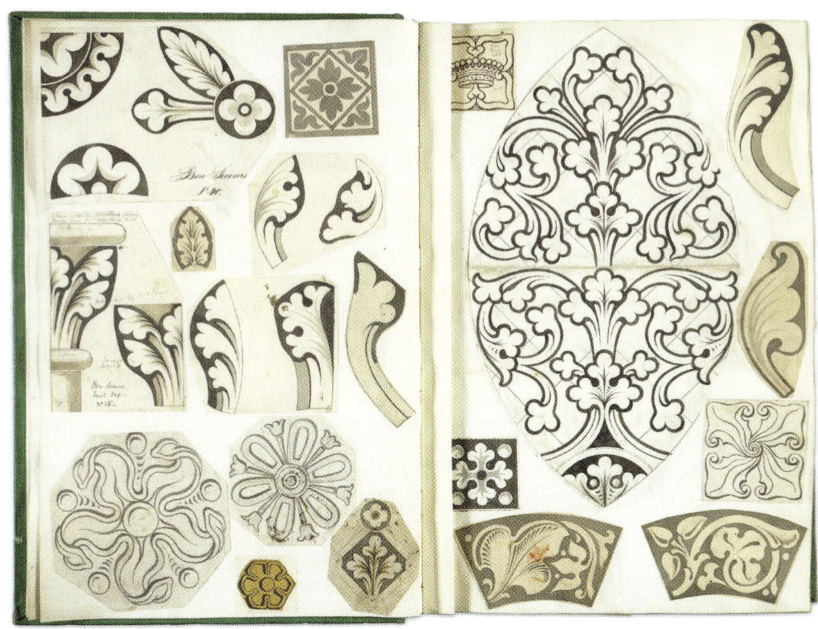

Fig. 16. Hunt *Decorative Designs* scrapbook, assembled ca. 1900.

collections were common to offices practicing eclectic design, but in the context of Richard Morris Hunt's collections, his photographs deepened cultural themes pictorially represented in his scrapbook series. We know from photographs that he hung architectural prints in his studios, but others, possibly scenic panoramas and views, were likely preserved at home as art.[33]

As a memorial to her late husband, Catharine Hunt brought Richard's photographs, scrapbooks, and books, from their houses and his studios, to the New York architectural office of their sons Richard H. and Joseph H. Hunt. There she arranged the collections alphabetically in custom cases and made them viewable by appointment, researchable with a four-volume catalog, including one dedicated to his renowned library of rare books. As an ensemble they represented an index of the very history museums were codifying through art objects. Together, they comprised what France's minister G. André Malraux foresaw in 1949 as the future, an Imaginary Museum (*Musée imaginaire*) of reproductions. Inspired by the grand encyclopedia enterprises

Fig. 17. Chester, England, photochrom mounted in Hunt album, assembled ca. 1900, Detroit Publishing Co., ca. 1890.

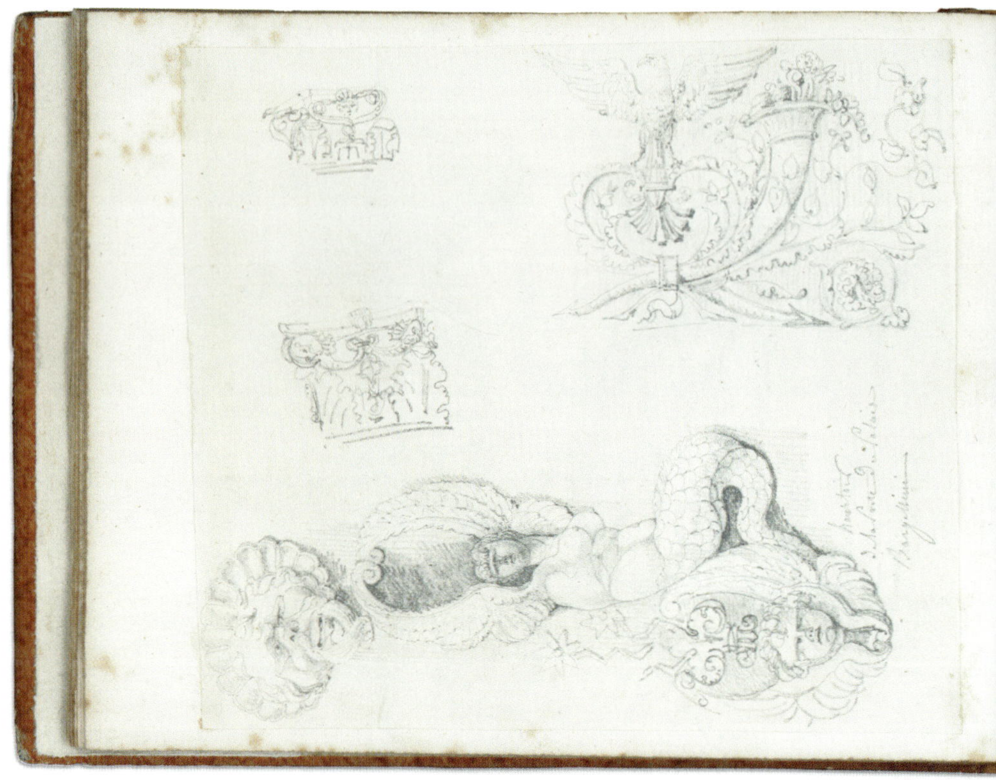

of their time, Richard Morris Hunt, assisted by Catharine, had created a virtual architectural museum.[34]

The *New York Times* obituary for Richard Morris Hunt reported that his library and "peerless collection of casts, drawings, and photographs" were destined for a public institution, probably one with collections that would augment and complete his own. As his sole heir, Catharine ultimately arranged for the AIA to receive Richard's library, scrapbooks, photographs, sketchbooks, and studio drawings, while retaining his three-dimensional art objects.[35]

As for Richard's casts, most were already at the Met by 1895. His donations had launched its collection of architectural details and scale models the year of the Fifth Avenue museum's opening in 1880, an undertaking supported by Henry G. Marquand, certainly with Hunt's

Fig. 18. Rare album of engravings of Bologna, with sketches by architect Antoine-François Callet, 1788, from the library of Richard M. Hunt.

guidance. Over the years Richard sent the Met casts of architecture from antiquity to the present, which he used from time to time to guide contractors in the proportions and quality he sought for his buildings.[36]

The public display of casts as exemplars of the world's finest art was a common practice in the nineteenth century. At Chicago's 1893 World's Columbia Exposition, where Hunt's gleaming Administrative Building welcomed over twenty-seven million visitors, the Met exhibited its model of the entrance to Alva Vanderbilt's Fifth Avenue chateau, likely donated to the museum by Hunt.[37] By assuring his own architecture was represented at the museum, and for that matter by photographs in the scrapbooks and folios given to the AIA, Richard Morris Hunt inscribed himself into the history of western art that he promoted to advance American culture.

Fig. 19.
Plaster model of
Fifth Avenue entrance,
William K. Vanderbilt
New York residence,
ca. 1893.

In my view, you cannot claim to have seen something until you have photographed it.

Émile Zola, *Collected Works*, 1901

USEUM catalogs and collections reveal that Catharine and Richard Hunt collected individually. They supported fundraising exhibitions and in the 1870s lent the Metropolitan Museum silver, pottery, furniture, ivories, and precious objects considered by Henry G. Marquand "a considerable portion" of early displays. When fine art became a focus in the 1880s, Richard sent the Met modern French paintings and Italian and Dutch old masters. Behind the scenes, Metropolitan staff discretely questioned the authenticity of some works, a not unexpected concern considering the market was rife with fakes, sometimes knowingly acquired by collectors and created by dealers themselves.[38]

In the utilitarian manner of a French atelier, with overtones of a South Kensington Museum gallery, Richard Morris Hunt placed casts, architectural photographs, and drawings in his studios to inform, educate, and inspire his assistants designing eclectic architecture.

From inventories and surviving images, we know that Richard and Catharine displayed paintings, sculpture, casts, and bibelots in their houses following a decorative style of the 1860s–1880s (see frontispiece). Though ascertaining the totality of their private collection and and its manner of display is challenging, 1916 photographs by architectural photographer Frances Benjamin Johnston of the Port Chester, New York house of Richard H. Hunt and the New York townhouse of Joseph H. Hunt provide clues. They show works owned by their parents and likely inherited after the death of their mother in 1909. As the two oldest children of Richard and Catharine, the brothers were logical heirs. They identified as collectors and were École des Beaux-Arts trained architects who continued their father's practice as Hunt & Hunt until 1924.[39]

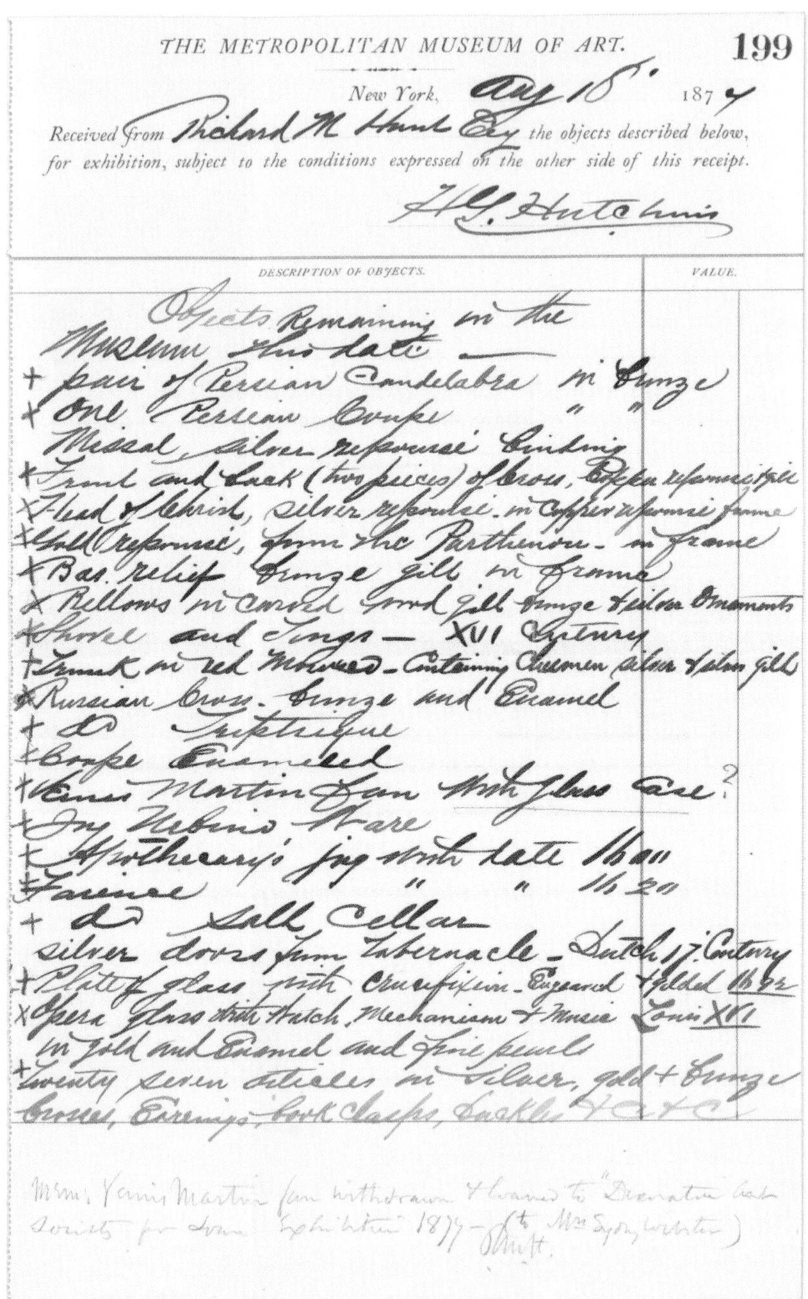

THE METROPOLITAN MUSEUM OF ART. **199**

New York, Aug 18th 1877

Received from Richard M Hunt Esq the objects described below, for exhibition, subject to the conditions expressed on the other side of this receipt.

H.G. Hutchins

DESCRIPTION OF OBJECTS.	VALUE.
Objects Remaining in the Museum this date —	
+ pair of Persian Candelabra in Bronze	
+ One Persian Coupe " "	
Missal, silver repoussé binding	
+ Front and back (two pieces) of Cross, Copper repoussé gilt	
+ Head of Christ, silver repoussé in Copper repoussé frame	
+ Gold repoussé, from the Parthenon — in frame	
+ Bas relief bronze gilt in frame	
+ Bellows in carved wood gilt bronze & silver Ornaments	
+ Shovel and Tongs — XVI Century	
+ Trunk in red Morocco — Containing [illegible] silver & silver gilt	
+ Russian Cross — bronze and Enamel	
+ do Triptique	
+ Coupe Enameled	
+ Vernis Martin Fan with glass case?	
+ Gy Urbino Ware	
+ Apothecary's jug with date 16[illegible]	
+ Faience " " 1620	
+ do Salt Cellar	
silver doors from Tabernacle — Dutch 17 Century	
+ Plate of glass with Crucifixion — Engraved & gilded 1692	
+ Opera glass with Watch, Mechanism & Music Louis XVI	
in gold and Enamel and fine pearls	
+ Twenty seven articles in Silver, gold & bronze	
Crosses, Earrings, book clasps, buckles &c &c	

Mem: Vernis Martin fan withdrawn & loaned to "Decorative Art Society for Loan Exhibition" 1877 — (to Mrs Sydney Webster) RMH.

Fig. 20. Richard M. Hunt loans to the Metropolitan Museum of Art, August 18, 1877.

Fig. 21. "The Studio," Richard H. Hunt residence, Acquehung Farm, Port Chester, New York (detail), Frances Benjamin Johnston, 1916.

A prominent room in the Johnston images is Richard H. Hunt's residential gallery called "The Studio," a term resonant with *studiolo,* the Renaissance domestic space for contemplative study. At the time Richard built the 40 x 28 foot room, ca. 1916, as an addition to his suburban house, decoration and display were spare. However, the objects, the Renaissance Revival architecture, and layered presentation of the Port Chester gallery were characteristic of spaces dating from the 1830s–1880s, known to Richard Morris Hunt in Paris (see Fig. 8) and New York. A notable example in America was the studio and gallery of the bric-a-brac collector par excellence, painter William Merritt Chase. His high-ceiling rooms were in Hunt's New York Tenth Street Studio

Fig. 22. *Studio Interior*, William Merritt Chase, ca. 1882.

Building (1858) where he himself had his office in the early 1860s (see Fig. 26).[40] A likely direct influence for the design of Richard H. Hunt's "Studio" was the gallery-atelier of the Viennese artist Hans Makart, easily known through images in the period and possibly in person by Richard Morris Hunt, who travelled to Austria and was friends with the country's eminent architect Friedrich von Schmidt. The American and Austrian rooms each have a distinctive Renaissance Revival antler pendant light, the Port Chester version having been commissioned from Viennese-born sculptor for Vanderbilt houses, Karl T.F. Bitter, who certainly knew of Makart's related fixture.[41]

Considering its limited seating and decorating style, consistent with earlier displays of bibelots, "The Studio" may have been conceived by Richard H. Hunt as a residential gallery of cognate arts, his own and the many collected by his parents.

As for Joseph H. Hunt, a journalist considered his New York townhouse "a museum" with "all kinds of bric-a-brac." Its reception room was furnished with a massive Renaissance Revival bookcase, "found in France," containing books and ornamented with "bibleots." This same piece appears in a stereoscope of the New York townhouse of Richard Morris

Fig. 23. Hans Makart studio, Vienna, Austria, Rudolf von Alt, 1895.

Fig. 24. Bookcase, reception room, Joseph H. Hunt residence, New York, Frances Benjamin Johnston, 1916.

Fig. 25.
Richard M. Hunt studio, Newport (detail), with casts, books, and fine art. Frank H. Child, ca. 1895.

Fig. 26. Richard M. Hunt studio, Studio Building, New York (detail), with photos, drawings, and casts, S. Beer, ca. 1861.

Hunt (see frontispiece) and may in fact be the "carved oak bookcase" he and Catharine Hunt lent to the Met in the 1870s and was possibly acquired by Richard as authentic during his student years in Paris.[42]

Today the bibelots and fine art owned by Catharine and Richard Hunt, including what they left to their sons, have been dispersed at auction and through inheritance. However, we know of several pieces in public collections: a silk textile from aristocratic France, beloved for its support of the American Revolution; a padlock and key from Paris's Bastille prison, loaned to a fundraiser for construction of the pedestal of the Statue of Liberty, designed by Richard Morris Hunt; a painting by Jean-François Millet of *Susannah and the Elders*; and a terrestrial globe dating to the era of Christopher Columbus. The rare Italian Renaissance object was a birthday present from Richard Morris Hunt to his client James Lenox, a fellow bibliophile and art collector for whom Richard designed the New York Lenox Library *cum* gallery (1877). Unaware of its rarity, Hunt had originally given the small copper ball to his children as a toy, a practice promoted by critics who considered fine and material arts at home, both period and in reproduction, as educational and socially refining.[43]

Fig. 27. *Susannah and the Elders*, Jean-François Millet, ca. 1846–1848, from the collection of Richard M. Hunt.

Fig. 28. Silk fragment, eighteenth century France, from the collection of Catharine H. Hunt.

Fig. 29. Italian copper globe, ca. 1508 [modern mount], from the collection of Richard M. Hunt.

The house was perversely full of souvenirs of places even more ugly than itself and of things it would have been a pious duty to forget.

Henry James, *Spoils of Poynton*, 1896

ICHARD Morris Hunt's collecting was integral to his success. Like students trained at the Met, he had learned from books and objects to design custom stone, metal, and wood decorations. This work advanced American design by educating his privileged clients and the artisans who carved, forged, cast, and embroidered The Gilded Age.[44]

Furthermore, Hunt's standing as a bibeloteur made him a credible authority in the closed society of patrons, architects, and designers who built and furnished the museums, libraries, and mansions that defined for the public "beauty" and "taste." In this, he and his clients laid the groundwork for the next generation of American collectors who filled the Met with fine art, an aspiration of trustees since 1870.[45]

Today, Richard Morris Hunt's legacy as a collector are his extant paper collections of over 15,000 items.[46] From the photographs, lists, loans, and accounts of his Washington Square days in New York discussed here, we know he also owned objects that he would have considered "cognate arts" related to architecture. Given the gestalt of his overall collection, a lingering question is why did Catharine Hunt exclude from her AIA donation the objects in Richard's collection? Was it to preserve this trove of bibelots as a family legacy? Or was a cultural force at work?

Richard Morris Hunt and his fellow collectors and museum founders believed that art would bring the respect they sought from peers in Europe, while securing the binding effects of what the influential critic Matthew Arnold defined in 1869 as "common" culture. By sharing the "best which has been thought and said in the world," in other words, in the history of western civilization, society would bring dignity to industrialized labor, thereby diminishing the threat of "anarchy" that

Fig. 30. Chancel tablets for All Souls Church (detail), Biltmore, North Carolina, Hunt office, ca. 1894.

loomed over societies recently prone to revolution.[47] But this is not how things turned out.

Limestone galleries and tree-lined boulevards of marbled mansions did not quell unrest, and by the time Richard Morris Hunt died, the utilitarian ideals of the mid-century museum and donor were blamed for encouraging "conspicuous consumption." Now institutions, under new leadership, ended their training programs and banished casts and applied arts.[48] New collectors and their allies, the museum curators, searched for exemplars of painting and sculpture, adding decorative arts, like William K. Vanderbilt's Marie-Antoinette furniture, exemplary for their beauty and provenance, not their practical use. Together the rich and poor would experience "art for art's sake" and what a museum director described as "the life of the imagination."[49] This profound shift made collections of "cognate arts" antiquarian, downgrading objects and furnishings Richard and Catharine Hunt collected to family mementos of their civilizing generation.

Fig. 31. Bronze candelabra, main hall (detail), The Breakers, Newport, Hunt office, "E.LM. February 1, 1894."

Fig. 32. Register grill (detail), Ochre Court, Newport, Hunt office, "MBC, Mar. 16/92".

Objects from the Richard M. Hunt Collection

Architecture

Gold repoussé from the Parthenon, Athens, in frame
Marble capital, Italian, sixteenth century
Piece of Moorish mosaic from Toledo, Spain
Piece of wall from the Alhambra, Spain

Bronze

Candelabra, Persian, pair [possibly brass] open work, engraved
Candelabra, Roman
Coupe, Persian
Lamp, Roman

Furnishings

Bellows in carved oak, chased gilt bronze, engraved silver ornament
Bookcase, carved oak [probably French Renaissance Revival]
Bookcase on chest "in the later style of Duncan Pyfe" [possibly from the collection of Jonathan Hunt Jr.]
Music stand, Dutch [also called folio stand]
Shovel and tongs, iron and brass, sixteenth century
Table, Louis XIII, oak

Glass and Pottery

Albarelli [earthenware jars] (2), dated 1510 and 1520
Boccaletto [pitcher]: Gubbio Lustre
Pitchers, Venetian, glass
Plate, glass, with crucifixion, engraved & gilded, 1592
Plates (10), Dutch, with scenes of a whaling voyage
Salt cellars (2), faience
Vase, Greek, terracotta, antique

Manuscripts

Book of Chinese costumes, in case
La [Chambre des] Comptes d'Innocent XI
Christ-glaubiger Seelen Heiligen-Fest-Andacht Schmuck, 1680, binding date 1721 (book on devotional jewelry)
German Gesangbuch (hymnal) dated 1764
Italian heraldry MSS.
Koran, in case
Missal with silver repoussé binding
Missal, Roman, very large, silver work on binding
Roger de Rabutin, Comte de Bussy MSS.
Tableaux Sacrés, 1594
Venetian MSS. on vellum

Miscellaneous

27 miscellaneous articles in silver, gold, and bronze: crosses, earrings, book clasps, buckles, crucifixes, medallions, etc. including: amulet (Swedish)
Amber mouthpiece of a Turkish chibouk
Arab sorbet spoon, wood
Bas relief, bronze gilt in frame
Box made of a 1732 French coin
Clock, Venetian, with gilt lion
Coupe, enameled
[Egyptian funerary] brick [stamped with] cone
Globe, copper, Italian Renaissance, ca. 1508 (New York Public Library as the Hunt-Lenox Globe)
Lock and key of the Bastille, iron
Opera glass with watch, Louis XV, mechanism & music, in gold and enamel and fine pearls
Print from copper plate-engraving on ivory plaque
Repoussé, copper, in ebony frame, Draped Venus with Cupid holding a quiver

Paintings, Drawings, and Sculpture

Paul-J.-A. Baudry, Venus and Cupid [color modello for salon ceiling, William K. Vanderbilt house, NYC]
Gustave Brion, Burial in the Black Forest [probably *A Funeral in the Vosges Mountains*, 1855]

Bust of Socrates, white marble, eighteenth century, Italian, after the antique
Thomas Couture, Sketch for the *Courtesan*
Thomas Couture, Portrait of Richard Morris Hunt, 1852 (National Portrait Gallery, Smithsonian, Washington, DC)
Frederic Crowninshield, sketch for a mural painting
Albert Cuyp, Horses
Narcisse Diaz de la Peña, Landscape
Louis Devereux, Chinese Warrior [probably not Chinese but Middle Eastern]
Giovanni di Licinio, Madonna painted on plaster [probably fresco]
Egyptian papyrus
Jean Gautherin, Portrait bust of Richard Morris Hunt, bronze, 1886 (Hunt Collection, Library of Congress)
[Jean-Léon] Gérôme, Study of a nude
Guercino da Cento, Christ in the Garden of Gethsemane [possibly *The Agony in the Garden*, Amguedda Cymu, Wales, UK]
Interior of St. Clements, Rome, watercolor
John La Farge, Flowers
Jean-François Millet, *Susannah and the Elders* (National Gallery of Victoria, Melbourne, Australia)
Painting on alabaster
[Pierre-Paul] Prud'hon, Venus and Cupid, sketch
Russian panels (2), of saints, on background of figured gold [probably icons]
David Teniers, A Kermesse
Unknown Dutch artist, Battle of the Thirty Years' War

Paintings and Sculpture by William Morris Hunt

Boy with a Butterfly, 1870 (Boston Atheneum)
Cupid Twanging his Bow, 1849-1850
Horses of Anahita or The Flight of Night, plaster of ca. 1848–1850 relief, cast probably by 1865 (Donated by Richard M. Hunt to the Metropolitan Museum of Art, 1880, probably from his own collection.)[50]
Lady and Child
Landscape
Mrs. Hutt [probably Catharine H. Hunt in *Mother and Child,* 1864–1865, Museum of Fine Arts, Boston].
The Singers [companion to *The Listeners*], ca. 1859
St. John, 1855 or 1874–1875.

Religious Objects

Assumption of the Virgin, painted on tortoise
Christ before Pilate, brass gilt repoussé
Crucifixion and Passion, Russian relief, champlevé enamel
Day of Pentecost, Russian relief in wood
Head of Christ, silver repoussé, copper repoussé frame
Processional Cross, antique Russian with rock-crystal and enamels
Processional Cross, front and back, copper gilt, repoussé
Virgin and Child, alabaster statuette

Silver

Brazil silver matté cup
Brazil silver matté tube [straw]
Chessmen, silver and gilt, in Morocco-leather box
Chinese pitcher
Coupes, pair
Doors of tabernacle, repoussé, Scenes of the Last Supper & Fall of Manna, seventeenth century, from a Dutch cathedral
Head ornament (Dutch)
Lady seated, cupid at her side, repoussé
Lamps
Mug, repoussé
Pair of cups, silver-gilt repoussé
Rosary, silver and ebony
Russian triptych of pheasants eating
Toilet brushes, etc., silver repoussé backs[51]

Objects from the Catharine H. Hunt Collection

Embroideries

The Annunciation, "very old"
Ecclesiastical embroidery with beads, unknown date
Embroidered and lace church curtain, Italian sixteenth century
Flight into Egypt, Holy Family, old French, French knots
Hold Family, silk threads sunk on parchment in wax
Moses and Miriam, Italian
St. Bartholomew, gold border
St. Elizabeth, "very old"
St. Françoise, French velvet frame with silver lace
St. Jerome, Florentine
St. John, Italian

Fans

Carved Chinese ivory, from the "First Empire"
Fan with pearl and gold sticks
French, with Chinese decoration
French, with Chinese decoration, Directoire
French, with inlaid shell sticks
Italian, with a pen and ink drawing of the Battle of the Amazons, seventeenth century
Spanish, with spangles
Vernis Martin, with glass case

Tapestry

Adoration of the Maji, 1520

Miscellaneous

Egg cups
Fragment, brocaded silk, 1700-1750 (Donated by Catharine H. Hunt to the Smithsonian-Cooper Hewitt, 1907)
Fragment, brocaded silk, eighteenth century (Donated by Catharine H. Hunt to the Smithsonian-Cooper Hewitt, 1907)
Fragment, silk, eighteenth century, France (Donated by Catharine H. Hunt to the Smithsonian-Cooper Hewitt, 1907)
Majolica plaque, the Virgin (the Immaculate Conception), Italian, 1620
Old hand glass [mirror]
Parisian curtains
Pin cushion

Paintings

Landscape, Listeners, Fontainebleau Forest, William Morris Hunt, 1850
Martin Brimmer, Sarah Wyman Whitman, 1892 (Donated by Catharine H. Hunt and the artist to Museum of Fine Arts, Boston, 1919)

Sources

The lists of Hunt objects are comprised of collectibles known from select catalogs, donations, and Met correspondence cited in the notes. They exclude objects from sketchbook lists and plaster casts purchased by Richard M. Hunt. The manuscripts are only those Richard exhibited from his extensive library.

1864: Metropolitan Fair, New York, in Georgeanna Muirson Woolsey and Eliza Woolsey Howland, *Letters of a Family During the* War, first published 1899, ed. Daniel John Hoisington (Roseville, Minnesota: 2001), 337

1877: Metropolitan Museum of Art Inventory, August 17, 1877 (Richard M. Hunt Collection, Library of Congress)

1878: Catalogue of the Loan Exhibition in Aid of the Society of Decorative Art...New York

1879: *Exhibition of the Works of William Morris Hunt*, Museum of Fine Arts, Boston

1880: Metropolitan Museum of Art, *Loan of Collection of Objects of Art...April to October*

1880: Metropolitan Museum of Art, *Loan Collection of Paintings...*

1883: *Pedestal Art Fund Exhibition, at the National Academy of Design*

1885: Metropolitan Museum of Art, *Loan Collection of Paintings...*

1885: Metropolitan Museum of Art, *Pictures by Old Masters...*

1887: Metropolitan Museum of Art, Inventories, November 16, 1887 (Richard Morris Hunt file, Met Archives)

1887: *Third Annual Exhibition of the Architectural League of New York*

1893: *World's Columbian Exhibition, Catalogue of New York State Loan Exhibit...*

1927: *The Collection of Richard Howland Hunt*...The Anderson Galleries, New York

Fig. 33. Paris Bastille prison padlock and its key, from the collection of Richard M. Hunt, 1883.

Notes

This sketchbook is published as a coda to Sam Watters, *The Gilded Life of Richard Morris Hunt* (2024), here cited as GL. For its extended notes, referenced here, and the Richard M. Hunt Collection at the Library of Congress, see https://guides.loc.gov/richard-morris-hunt; here as HLOC.

1 Walter Benjamin, "Paris, Hauptstadt des 19. Jahrhunderts," 1938, is the title of one of two completed essays Benjamin wrote in preparing his *Arcades Project.*
2 James Wynne, *Private Libraries of New York* (New York: E. French, 1860), 269, 278.
3 Wynne, 279; Henry Van Brunt, "Richard Morris Hunt," *Proceedings of the Twenty-Ninth Annual Convention of the American Institute of Architects* (1895): 75; William H. Wight, "Richard Morris Hunt," *The Inland Architect and News Record* 26, no. 1 (August 1895): 2.
4 GL, 117.
5 GL, 174.
6 The specificity and personal nature of the purchases listed in Richard Morris Hunt's sketchbooks and, in cases, their appearance in later inventories and photographs, their consistency with purchases in his École-years, and that his sketchbooks make no reference to purchases for clients, confirms these 1867 acquisitions were personal, with some casts donated to the Met after its founding in 1870.
7 For the 1867 purchases, see Richard Morris Hunt sketchbook, 1867, S79.23, HLOC; for Désachy for Marble House design, see GL, 218.
8 "*Une armée de collectionneurs jeunes... les armes, les meubles, l'orfèverie, les tappiseries, les émaux, les faïences....*" in Edmond Bonnaffé, *Le Musée Spitzer* (Paris: Imprimerie d'Art, 1890), 9.
9 Janell Watson, *Literature and Material Culture from Balzac to Proust* (Cambridge: Cambridge University Press, 1999), 23.
10 GL, 47, 59; Félix Mornand, "Principaux hôtels de Paris: L'hôtel de Mademoiselle Rachel," *L'Illustration* 22 (September 3, 1853): 155 as quoted in Watson, 73; Hunt on du Sommerard, as quoted in Wynne, 270–71.
11 GL, 68.
12 Noah Webster, Chauncey A. Goodrich, Noah Porter, *An American Dictionary of the English Language...* (Springfield, MA: GL and C. Mirriam, 1862), 208; Hunt, 1893 to the Architectural League of New York, as quoted in GL, 273.
13 GL, 70.
14 "Address by Richard M. Hunt, President of the New York Chapter," *Proceedings of Second Annual Convention of the American Institute of Architects* (1869): 153; see also 151–52.
15 Ibid., 154.
16 Ibid., 154; as quoted in Julius Bryant, *Creating the V & A, Victoria and Albert's Museum (1851–1861)* (London: Lund Humphries in association with V & A Publishing, 2019), 44; see also 28–33, 127–31. For an overview of South Kensington's influence, Steven Conn, *Museums and American Intellectual Life, 1876–1926* (Chicago and London: University of Chicago Press, 1999), 195–205. The impact of the museum extended into American education, through Walter Smith (1836–1888),

graduate of the South Kensington School of Art and a prominent industrial arts educator in Boston from 1871.

17 *A Metropolitan Art-Museum in the City of New York* (New York: Art Committee of the Union League Club of New York, 1869), 3.

18 Ibid., 4, 12–18; C.C. Cole, Professor George Fiske Comfort, and editor William Cullen Bryant gave the meeting the gravitas required to raise funds.

19 For AIA members, see GL, 30–31. Quoted from an 1870 report by a subcommittee of the Art Committee of the Union League Club, advisor to the museum founders, in Winifred Howe, *A History of the Metropolitan Museum of Art*, vol. 1 (New York: The Metropolitan Museum of Art, 1913), 122; see same page for what constituted educational works: "drawings, engravings, medals, photographs, architectural models, historical portraits," all categories Richard M. Hunt envisioned for his architectural museum.

20 For Richard M. Hunt loans to the museum at opening, see catalog, *Metropolitan Museum of Art, Loan Collection of Objects of* Art (April–October, 1880): 12, 23–24, 30–31, 32, 24; Choate, quoted in Howe, 198–99. Hunt worked on securing contributions before 1880; see Paul R. Baker, *Richard Morris Hunt* (Cambridge: MIT Press, 1984), 178; and was for one year on the Met's "Loan Exhibition Committee," loans being central to the museum's early success and much discussed by trustees, citing the South Kensington Museum and lack of American government support. *Annual Report of the Trustees of the Association* (1873): 3; and 1872 annual report: 12.

21 Hunt's first collector was Mayor William P. Wright (ca. 1865), for whom he built a residential gallery in New Jersey; then William H. Osborn (1870) in New York, a patron of the Met, and in Boston, Martin Brimmer (1870), a collector and lender to the Met, and a founder in 1870 of Boston's Museum of Fine Arts, indebted to the South Kensington Museum; in Chicago Hunt designed the house (1873) of museum patron and bibeloteur Marshall Field, see GL, 67–68, 118–23, and related extended notes, online, HLOC; for Brimmer and the Met, see its Annual Report (1872), op. cit.: 13.

22 For Hunt purchasing for Henry G. Marquand, see GL, 170, note 35.

23 *Metropolitan Museum of Art, Eleventh Annual Report of the Trustees of the Association* (1881): 10–12.

24 Ibid., GL, 117.

25 GL, 170–74; Decoration by period was well established at home and abroad, and a factor in converting house to museum; see for instance Enrico Colle, "In the Heart of Florentine Collections: Frederick Stibbert and His Museum," *The Evolving House Museum: Art Collectors and Their Residences, Then and Now,* ed. Margaret Iacono Wertz Esmée Quodbach (Leiden: Koninklijke Brill BVGL, 2024), 80–110, with essays on The Frick Collection and The John and Mabel Ringling Museum of Art; see HLOC for photographs of the Marquand houses.

26 For European collections and the Vanderbilts, see GL, 236–38; "*un magasin de curiosités,*" "*bibloterie écrasante,*" Goncourt, September 29, 1872, *Journal*, vol. 2. ed. Robert Ricatte (Paris: Fasquelle and Flammarion, 1956), 531.

27 For houses as educative and civilizing, see GL, 158–59, 174, 218. An inspiration for Alva Vanderbilt was Hunt's 1878–79 New York client, Egerton L. Winthrop, who straddled the bibeloteur to connoisseur divide, GL, 154–58; for her Fifth Avenue house, GL, 163–66; William K. Vanderbilt's bequest was in 1920; for Cornelius as patron see note 36.

28 For the gothic room, see *Gothic Art in the Gilded Age*, ed. Virginia Brilliant (Sarasota, FL: The John and Mable Ringling Museum of Art, 2009); for the bell and bottle, see pp. 101, 147.

29 For another bibeloteur in the 1860–70s, see Alexander Petrovitch Basilewsky, whose collection was considered a private museum, the "musée Basilewsky," focusing on the Middle Ages and Renaissance, Frédéric Tixier, "Un Certain Goût pour l'Orfèverie Mosane au XIXe Siècle: Quelques Remarques sur la Collection Parisienne d'Alexandre

Basilewsky," *Orfèverie Septentrionale, XIIe et XIIIe Siècle*, ed. Philippe George (Liège: Trésor de la Cathédrale, 2016), 121–138. Edmond Bonnaffé distinguished Spitzer from du Sommerard, Sauvageot, and the Russian-Parisian bibeloteur Prince Peter Soltykoff (auction of his collection, Hôtel Drouot, 1861) for his rigorous collecting and display; Le Musée Spitzer, 148–50. For Spitzer and Gavet in Hunt-designed houses, see GL, 211, 218, 222. See Paris dealer Henri J. Stettiner invoice to Ogden Goelet for windows from the Spitzer sale, July 10, 1893; Roy G. Thomas [the window restorer] to Robert W. Goelet, August 4, 1936 and related correspondence, series 3, Goelet Family Papers, Salva Regina University, Newport, RI.

30 Anne Higonnet, *A Museum of One's Own* (New York: Periscope, 2009), 14–16.

31 Catharine H. Hunt, unpublished biography of Richard M. Hunt (ca. 1905), binder 3, 334, HLOC.

32 Arthur Penn, *The Home Library* (New York: D. Appleton and Company, 1883), 13–14; *The Scrapbook in American Life*, ed. Susan Tucker, Katherine Ott, and Patricia P. Buckler (Philadelphia: Temple University Press, 2006).

33 Contemporaneous collections are approximately 3500 architectural photos, formerly in 53 volumes, assembled by Henry H. Richardson (Frances Loeb Library, Harvard University, Cambridge, MA, donated 1936); and The Russell Sturgis Photograph Collection of approximately 15,000 photos of architecture, painting, sculpture and archeological sites (Washington University Library, St. Louis, MI, acquired 1909). Though both collections had related book libraries, there is no record of either including scrapbooks like Hunt's visual encyclopedia. A contemporaneous architect-collector who straddled the transition from bibeloteur to connoisseur was Stanford White, see Wayne Craven, *Stanford White, Decorator in Opulence and Dealer in Antiquities* (New York: Columbia University Press, 2005).

34 One display cabinet is in the HLOC; for the organizing of the collection by Catharine Hunt, see GL, 99, 267 and associated notes; the bound catalogs are in the HLOC; Malraux introduced the term in *Psychologie d'Art* (1947), revised as *Les Voix du Silence.* (1951); an encyclopedic enterprise that was in essence a published scrapbook was the series *Matériaux et documents d'architecture et de sculpture,* Paris, 1872–1914; another undertaking certainly known to Richard Morris Hunt which combined publishing and a print museum, was by his École colleague and collaborator in the William K. Vanderbilt New York house, designer Émile-Auguste Reiber who published his *Albums-Reiber, Bibliothèque portative des Arts du Dessin* (Paris: Ateliers du Musée-Reiber, 1877); for collaboration, GL, 166.

35 "Death of Richard Morris Hunt," *The New York Times,* August 1, 1895. At the turn of the century, Catharine Hunt committed to the donation on the prompting of the AIA, then building an historical archive of important members. GL, 267, and related extended note, online, HLOC. See also correspondence at the Library of Congress in the Prints & Photographs division. For an extensive note regarding the transfer of the collections to the AIA, see Afterword, note 9, para. 7, in extended notes to GL, online, HLOC.

36 Hunt's 1880 donation was "a large and fine collection of casts of works of art, ancient and modern, which has already proved its uses in our [the Met's] technical schools, and will be of permanent value for the study of artists and artisans;" that same year Hunt's client Cornelius Vanderbilt II donated seven-hundred old master drawings, *Metropolitan Museum of Art, Eleventh Annual Report*, 1881, 13; also *Catalogue of Collection of Casts,* 2nd ed. (New York: Metropolitan Museum of Art, 1910), vii–viii. The Met sold and donated their plaster collections in the 1980s. For using casts, GL, 218.

37 For loan, see chapter 5, note 60, GL extended notes, online, HLOC. The model was exhibited in Chicago with architectural drawings by Richard M. Hunt's contemporaries.

38 For loans to charities and the Met, see GL, 117, 204; for inventories, see GL extended notes HLOC, chapter 3, note 35, chapter 5, note 7, and here, Fig. 20; for Marquand, *Metropolitan Museum of Art Twenty-Sixth Annual Report of the Trustees of the Association* (1896): 12. The inventory of fifty-one objects, paintings, and furniture returned by the Met to the Hunts in November 1887 probably reflects close to the totality of what they had lent, exempting their old masters, and was being returned as the museum pivoted towards fine art; see File: Hunt, Richard Morris, 1869, 1871, 1890..., Institutional Archive, Metropolitan Museum of Art. For the authenticity of Hunt works of art, see in this file letter, Isaac H. Hall to Luigi di Cesnola, November 4, 1887.

Navigating between what was considered private and of public interest, Catharine in her biography of Richard acknowledged only two sources of their collections, the Hôtel Drouot and a Bologna dealer, Alessandro Ascoli; GL chapter 5, notes 7 and 13, extended notes online, HLOC. Some circles thought bibelot collecting, dominated by sales at the Hôtel Drouot, detrimental to contemporary art, a point debated by Edmond Bonnaffé, defender of Spitzer and collectors mentioned here, see his *Collectionneurs de l'ancienne France* (Paris: Auguste Aubry, 1873), iv. The subject of fakes is nuanced, with dealers knowingly peddling reproductions and restored works. The collector Arabella Huntington and founder of a house museum, owned a fake Boulle desk. Because of this, she was convinced to sell it, astonishingly by its original dealer. Regretting her decision, she bought it back. "I like that desk and I don't care whether it is original or not," she told a friend. Arnold Genthe, *As I Remember* (New York: Reynal & Hitchcock, 1936), 153.

39 For a French atelier, see GL, 38. Early in his career Hunt taught students in his studio and was a lifetime promoter of architectural education. See GL 69–70. For objects owned by Richard and Catharine Hunt, which included the painting *Mother and Child* by William Morris Hunt (see Fig. 21) and a portrait of Richard Morris Hunt by Thomas Couture, visible in photographs of the Richard H. and Joseph H. Hunt houses, see GL, dust jacket, 2, 79, 81, 205, and below, note 41, Fessenden. The will of Richard Morris Hunt stipulated that all his possessions were the property of his wife until her death when they were to be divided among their children. For this, see Will of Richard Morris Hunt, HLOC, and relatedly, Afterword, note 9, extended notes to GL, online, HLOC.

40 De Witt H. Fessenden, "Two Architects and Their Homes," *The International Studio* 62, no. 247 (September 1917): LXXIV; GL, 56–57. Chase's Spanish *Bric-a-Brac Shop* 1883 at the de Young Museum, San Francisco captures the look of galleries the artist had seen on an 1882 trip and which Hunt would have experienced while shopping in Spain four years later, see GL, 192. For curiosities from this trip, see Chase's loans in the *Pedestal Art Fund Exhibition, at the National Academy of Design, December 1883*, which also includes loans from Richard and Catharine Hunt individually (see here Fig. 33).

41 For pendant light, *The Collection of Richard Howland Hunt, American and Italian Furniture, Tapestries, Textiles, and Needlework, Pictures, Pewter, Japanese Armor, Etc. Including Many Heirlooms of the Hunt Family Removed from "The Studio" at Portchester, New York to be Sold by Mr. Hunt's Order*, Anderson Galleries, March 26, 1927: 56, lot 154, illustrated, as "Carved suspension in the German Renaissance Taste..." and made for "Mr. Hunt" by Bitter, a sculptor who worked for Richard Morris Hunt at Marble House, The Breakers, and Biltmore; a published source for the Makart studio, as well as studios by artists known to Richard Morris Hunt, including Paul Baudry, was *Modern Artists..., prepared under the direction of F.G. Dumas* (London: JS Virtue and Co, ca. 1880–82). For von Schmidt, see 1867 sketchbook, S79.25, HLOC.

The extent to which the Richard H. and Joseph H. Hunt interiors were furnished with arts from their parents is indeterminate.

Fessenden portrays the brothers as avid collectors, with no mention of their owning objects from their parents, which was not the case. In fact, it is likely the displayed objects were largely inherited, given their aspect, what Catharine and Richard Hunt collected, and that arts mentioned in the article look and are described like ones Catharine and Richard Morris Hunt owned. To date no record has been found of the brothers making loans to public institutions, an activity that would have been consistent with Fessenden's hyperbolic portrait. This inheritance and possibly interiors of Richard Morris Hunt homes may have determined the dated decorating of the brothers' interiors. For a discussion of the inheritance, in relation to the Richard H. Hunt "Studio" auction, cited above, see chapter 2, note 4, in extended notes to GL, online, HLOC.

42 Cornice of bookcase removed by Joseph H. Hunt. Fessenden, LXXI–LXXII; for purchase in Paris and the bookcase's provenance from "the hotel of a foreign ambassador," see Catharine H. Hunt, unpublished biography, binder 1, 28. HLOC; for its loan to the Met, see November 15, 1887 inventory letter to Richard Morris Hunt, File, Institutional Archive, the Met, op. cit. For another view of the Joseph H. Hunt reception room, see "Portfolio of Current Architecture," *Architectural Record* 49, no. 15 (September, 1916): 259; also illustrated here is a bedroom in the Louis XV style, reflecting the taste of 1916, versus the "bibelot" taste of the dining and reception rooms.

43 For this see, GL, 110, and related extended note, online, HLOC.

44 See the *In Memoriam* written by the workers at Biltmore for Catharine H. Hunt, on the death of her husband, GL, 264–65; and the document itself, HLOC.

45 A client influenced by Hunt on many fronts was George W. Vanderbilt, who collected engravings, books, casts, and architectural photographs he pasted into albums.

46 For a discussion of the collection contents and quantities, see HLOC online profile.

47 Matthew Arnold, *Culture and Anarchy*, 2nd ed. (London: Smith, Elder, and Co., 1882), x, first published 1869, a year before the founding of the Met and Museum of Fine Arts, Boston.

48 For the decline of cast collections, see Alan Wallach, *Exhibiting Contradictions: Essays on the Art Museum in the United States* (Amherst: University of Massachusetts Press, 1998), 38–54.

49 Matthew Pritchard Benjamin Gilman, *Museum Ideals of Purpose and Method* (Boston: Boston Museum of Fine Arts, 1923), 95, as quoted in Andrew McClellan, *The Art Museum From Boullée to Bilbao* (Berkeley, Los Angeles, and London: University of California Press, 2008), 28–29, where McClellan points to J. Pierpont Morgan, a bibeloteur of a high order, elected president of the Met in 1909, as moving the museum towards fine art; in this regard see also Conn, 197–98. It is of note that William K. Vanderbilt *donated* his fine paintings and French court furniture to the Met on his death in 1920, while his former wife Alva *sold* her bibelot-dominant Gavet collection in the 1920s, perhaps because such objects were no longer sought by established museums, but had a gilded provenance of interest to John Ringling, who, similarly, purchased paneling from the Richard M. Hunt-designed, Fifth Avenue double house of Caroline S. Astor. See GL, chapter 6, note 18, extended notes online, HLOC.

50 See here frontispiece, Hunt parlor, by bookcase, a cast of the Anahita relief.

51 For Richard M. Hunt's interest in metalwork as artisanal, see GL, 117; for other works collected by Hunt, see his 1852–53 sketchbooks, HLOC.

Image Credits

Frontispiece: Richard M. Hunt Collection, Library of Congress, LC-DIG-ppmsca-74923

Title Page: Table for Main Hall, Biltmore (detail), 1895. Richard M. Hunt Collection, Library of Congress, LC-DIG-ppmsca-53471

Table of Contents: Richard M. Hunt Collection, Library of Congress, LC-DIG-ppmsca-89709

Fig. 1: Richard M. Hunt Collection, Library of Congress, LC-DIG-ppmsca-73359

Fig. 2: BTEU/RKMLGE/Alamy Ltd.

Fig. 3: Richard M. Hunt Collection, Library of Congress, LC-DIG-ppmsca-57032

Fig. 4: Victoria & Albert Museum, London: 2023NL2386

Fig. 5: Richard M. Hunt Collection, Library of Congress, LC-DIG-ppmsca-89701

Fig. 6: Richard M. Hunt Collection, Library of Congress, LC-DIG-ppmsca-89702

Fig. 7: Musée du Louvre; © RMN-Grand Palais / Art Resource, New York

Fig. 8: Alexandre and Edmond du Sommerard, *Les Arts du Môyen Âge*, Atlas volume, 1846, Richard M. Hunt Collection, Library of Congress, LC-DIG-ppmsca-95790

Fig. 9: Victoria & Albert Museum, London: 2010EH3054

Fig. 10: Victoria & Albert Museum, London: 2011EW6379

Fig. 11: Metropolitan Museum of Art

Fig. 12: Found at Chateau-sur-Mer. Courtesy of Michael Froio, Michael-Froio.com.

Fig. 13: George W. Sheldon, *Artistic Houses*, vol.2, part 1, New York, 1884, General Collection, Library of Congress, LC-DIG-ppmsca-56277

Fig. 14: The Preservation Society of Newport County, found at Marble House

Fig. 15: Émile Molinier, *Collection Émile Gavet: Catalogue Raisonné Precédé d'une Étude Historique et Archéologique sur Les Oeuvres d'Art qui Composent Cette Collection*, Paris, 1889, Richard M. Hunt Collection, Library of Congress, LC-DIG-ppmsca-68591

Fig. 16: Richard M. Hunt Collection. Library of Congress, LC-DIG-ppmsca-89715

Fig. 17: Richard M. Hunt Collection, Library of Congress, LC-DIG-ppmsca-74925

Fig. 18: Leather-bound volume of engravings of Bologna, assembled by architect Antoine-Françoise Callet, with related sketches, 1788, owned by his son, the architect, Félix-Emmanuel Callet, Richard M. Hunt Collection, Library of Congress, LC-DIG-ppmsca-73358

Fig. 19: Richard M. Hunt Collection, Library of Congress, LC-DIG-ppmsca-53515

Fig. 20: Richard M. Hunt Collection, Library of Congress, LC-DIG-ppmsca-98072

Fig. 21 Frances Benjamin Johnston Collection, Library of Congress, LC-DIG-ppmsca-56270

Fig. 22: Brooklyn Museum, Gift of Mrs. Carl H. de Silver in memory of her husband

Fig. 23: Wien Museum, Erich Lessing / Art Resource, New York

Fig. 24: Richard M. Hunt Collection, Library of Congress, LC-DIG-ppmsca-98073

Fig. 25: Richard M. Hunt Collection, Library of Congress, LC-DIG-ds-10184

Fig. 26: Richard M. Hunt Collection, Library of Congress, LC-DIG-ppmsca-98085

Fig. 27: National Gallery of Victoria, Melbourne, Victoria, Australia

Fig. 28: Cooper Hewitt, Smithsonian Museum of Design, New York, 1907 Gift -20-15-a/f

Fig. 29: New York Public Library, NY

Fig. 30: Richard M. Hunt Collection, Library of Congress, LC-DIG-ppmsca-98083

Fig. 31: Richard M. Hunt Collection. Library of Congress, LC-DIG-ppmsca-74974

Fig. 32: Richard M. Hunt Collection. Library of Congress, LC-DIG-ppmsca-88676

Fig. 33: *Pedestal Art Fund Exhibition, at the National Academy of Design*, December, 1883

With Appreciation

Erica Esau, Michael Froio, Paul Micio,
Mari Nakahara, David S. Rodes, Valeska, and
The Preservation Society of Newport County.

KETCHBOOKS were nineteenth-century iPads, portable volumes for recording what caught the eye and mind of artists and architects as they traveled and studied the globe, made accessible by the modern steamer and railroad.

Similar to ones kept by Richard Morris Hunt over thirty-five years of international travel, this small book is designed for an interactive experience like his own, with blank pages for annotations, comments, and sketches as you experience the Gilded-Age world of Richard Morris Hunt—in Newport, New York, Biltmore, and beyond.

Drawings on the pages for sketching are excerpted from Richard Morris Hunt sketchbooks, visible online at the Library of Congress.

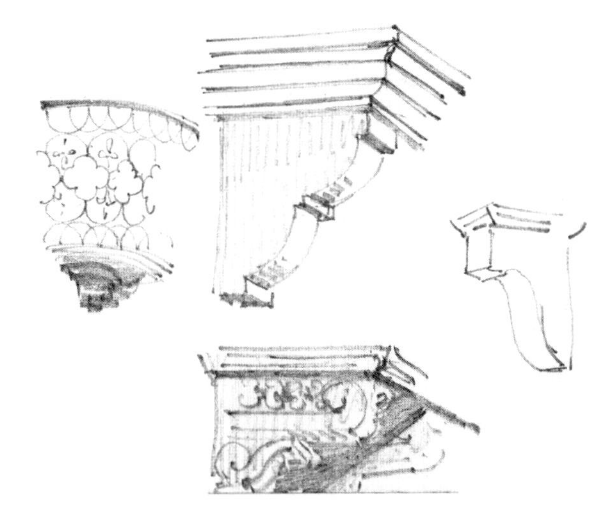

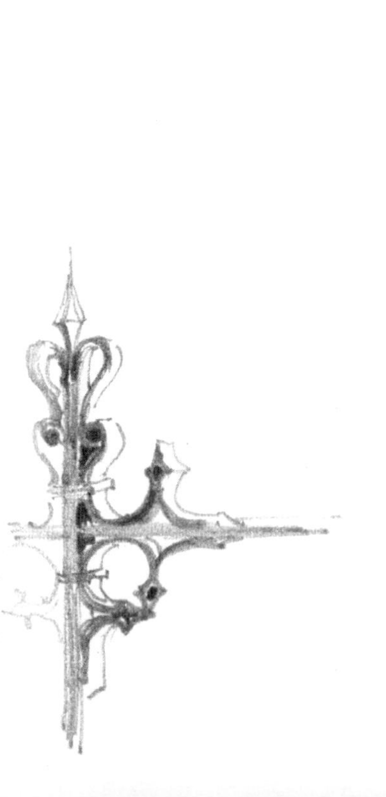

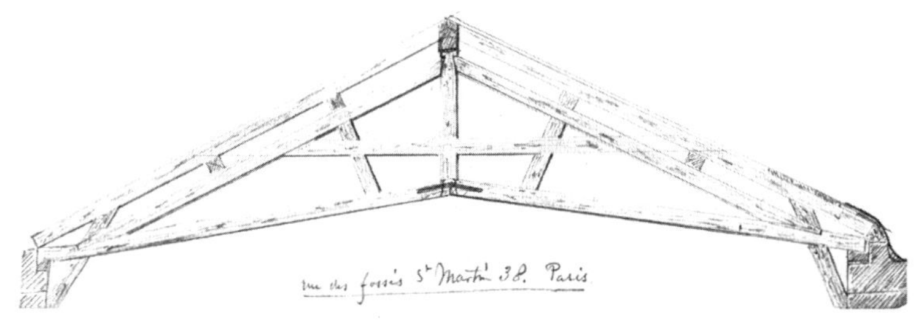
rue des fossés St Martin 38. Paris

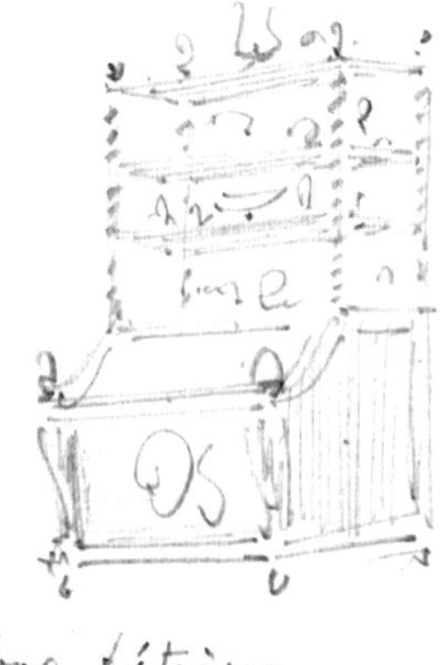

Wood box & étagère

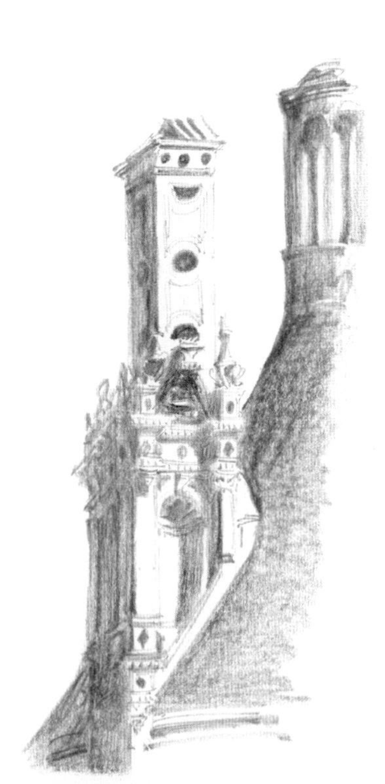